OHIO

Val Lawton

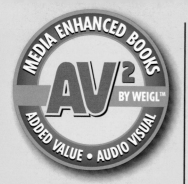

AV² provides enriched content that supplements and complements this book. Weigl's AV² books strive to create inspired learning and engage young minds in a total learning experience.

Your AV² Media Enhanced books come alive with...

Audio
Listen to sections of the book read aloud.

Key Words
Study vocabulary, and complete a matching word activity.

Video
Watch informative video clips.

Quizzes
Test your knowledge.

Embedded Weblinks
Gain additional information for research.

Slide Show
View images and captions, and prepare a presentation.

Try This!
Complete activities and hands-on experiments.

... and much, much more!

Go to **www.av2books.com**, and enter this book's unique code.

BOOK CODE

N343953

AV² by Weigl brings you media enhanced books that support active learning.

Published by AV² by Weigl
350 5th Avenue, 59th Floor
New York, NY 10118
Website: www.av2books.com

Library of Congress Cataloging-in-Publication Data
Names: Lawton, Val, author.
Title: Ohio : the Buckeye State / Val Lawton.
Description: New York, NY : AV2 by Weigl, 2015. | Series: Discover America | Includes index.
Identifiers: LCCN 2015047958 (print) | LCCN 2015048748 (ebook) | ISBN 9781489649201 (hard cover : alk. paper) | ISBN 9781489649218 (soft cover : alk. paper) | ISBN 9781489649225 (Multi-User eBook)
Subjects: LCSH: Ohio--Juvenile literature.
Classification: LCC F491.3 .L394 2015 (print) | LCC F491.3 (ebook) | DDC 977.1--dc23
LC record available at http://lccn.loc.gov/2015047958

Printed in the United States of America, in Brainerd, Minnesota
1 2 3 4 5 6 7 8 9 0   20 19 18 17 16

042016
040816

Project Coordinator Heather Kissock
Art Director Terry Paulhus

Photo Credits
Every reasonable effort has been made to trace ownership and to obtain permission to reprint copyright material. The publisher would be pleased to have any errors or omissions brought to their attention so that they may be corrected in subsequent printings. The publisher acknowledges Getty Images, Corbis Images, iStock, and Alamy as its primary image suppliers for this title.

OHIO

Contents

STATE BIRD
Cardinal

STATE FLAG
Ohio

STATE TREE
Ohio Buckeye

STATE ANIMAL
White-tailed Deer

STATE FLOWER
Scarlet Carnation

STATE SEAL
Ohio

Nickname
The Buckeye State

Motto
With God, All Things
Are Possible

Song
"Beautiful Ohio," by Ballard
MacDonald and Mary Earl

Population
(2014 Census est.) 11,594,163
Ranked 7th state

Entered the Union
March 1, 1803, as the 17th state

Capital
Columbus

Discover Ohio

Ohio is a remarkable state, with rich farmland, beautiful scenery, exciting cities, and a well-preserved history. It is part of the central heartland region of the United States called the Midwest. Ohio borders Michigan and Lake Erie to the north. Kentucky and West Virginia are across the Ohio River to the south and southeast. Indiana is to the west, and Pennsylvania is to the east.

Hiking, camping, fishing, and horseback riding are all available in Ohio's 74 state parks. Columbus, Cleveland, and Cincinnati are the three major cities in the state. Not only are they important to the state's economics, but they also feature major league sports teams, major universities, and maintain a rich culture steeped in history.

The state is known for its fertile plains and rolling hills, but the state is also famous for the Rock and Roll Hall of Fame and Museum in Cleveland. The museum showcases rock and roll's great artists, such as Elvis Presley, the Beatles, Elton John, and Aretha Franklin. Ohio even has an official rock song, "Hang on Sloopy." It was a hit in 1965 for a group from Dayton, the McCoys.

The Land

Columbus, Ohio, sits on the Scioto River. The Scioto Mile is an urban park that connects downtown with 145 acres of parkland.

On April 1, 1853, Cincinnati established the **first professional fire department** in the nation.

About **half of the U.S. population** lives within a **500-mile radius** of Columbus, Ohio.

With easy access to trade, Cincinnati grew along the Ohio River. The river gave the city a variety of economic opportunities.

Beginnings

People have lived on the land that is now Ohio for at least 11,000 years. By the 1700s, Native Americans from areas in New England had begun to settle in what is now Ohio. They were attracted by the area's abundant land and **game**.

The first group of Europeans to live in the Ohio area were French fur traders. The British took control of the area in the mid-1700s after the French and Indian War. Settlers looking to farm the land soon made their way into Ohio. Before the 1800s, most farmers supported their families by growing and selling grain.

Throughout the state's history, the Ohio River and Lake Erie have been important transportation routes. Toledo and Cleveland are major shipping ports on Lake Erie. Cincinnati, in the southwestern part of the state, expanded around its busy river port on the Ohio River. At several points along the Ohio River, ferries transport cargo and passengers between Ohio and neighboring states.

Where is OHIO?

Ohio is mostly surrounded by water, making up much of the state's borders. The Lake Erie shoreline runs for 312 miles to the north, and there are eight ports along the lake in Ohio. Meanwhile, the Ohio River, which is one of the largest rivers in North America, flows for more than 450 miles along the state's southern and southeastern borders. Ohio has more than 3,300 named rivers and streams, and more than 60,000 lakes, **reservoirs**, and ponds.

United States Map

Ohio

Alaska   Hawai'i

INDIANA

MAP LEGEND

- ◻ Ohio
- ☆ Capital City
- ● Major City
- 🏞 Cuyahoga Valley National Park
- ▲ Stan Hywet Hall and Gardens
- ◻ Bordering States
- ◻ Canada
- ◻ Water

N

SCALE   0   50 miles

KENTUCKY

1 Columbus

Columbus became the state capital of Ohio in 1816. Before that time, the towns of Chillicothe and Zanesville had both served as the capital. Columbus was chosen as the site for the new capital because of its central location within the state and access to major river routes. It is the largest city in Ohio.

2 Cleveland

The state's second largest city, Cleveland has a population of more than 380,000. Visitors can enjoy the culture of Cleveland with the Cleveland Museum of Art, Botanical Gardens, and the Cleveland West Side Market. The city is also the manufacturing hub of Ohio.

Lake Erie

Cleveland

2

4

3

PENNSYLVANIA

OHIO

Columbus

1

WEST VIRGINIA

3 **Stan Hywet Hall and Gardens**

Located in Akron, Ohio, the Stan Hywet Hall and Gardens belonged to F. A. Seiberling, the founder of Goodyear Tire and Rubber Company. The term "Stan Hywet" is Old English for "stone quarry." Today, visitors can tour the estate, which includes the home, gardens, conservatory, and gate lodge.

4 **Cuyahoga Valley National Park**

Cleveland and Akron are both a short distance from Cuyahoga Valley National Park. The valley shows signs of having more than 12,000 years of human occupation. Since the late 1990s, the park has rehabilitated historic farmsteads and leased the farmsteads to farmers who use **sustainable** practices.

Land Features

The three major land regions of Ohio are the Appalachian Plateau, the Lake Plains, and the Central Plains, which are also called the Till Plains. The Appalachian Plateau is an area of winding rivers, hills, and hardwood trees that reaches west from Ohio's eastern border. The slightly rolling Lake Plains, in the northwestern part of the state, extend along Lake Erie to the Michigan border. The Central Plains, in central-western and southwestern Ohio, provide deep, fertile soil. This region is part of the nation's Corn Belt.

Thousands of years ago, **glaciers** blanketed about two-thirds of the area that is now Ohio, shaping the land into gently rolling hills as they moved across it. The melting glaciers left swamps and bogs, especially in the northwestern part of the state. Later, when the areas were drained by natural processes or by settlers, fertile soil remained.

Hocking Hills State Park

This park, in the south-central part of the state, is popular with hikers. The park features spectacular rock formations, deep gorges, cliffs, and waterfalls.

Kelleys Island

Located in Lake Erie, Kelleys Island is known for its unique natural features. They include a limestone cobble beach and abundant red cedar trees.

Cuyahoga Valley National Park

The only national park in Ohio, Cuyahoga Valley, in the northeast, has waterfalls, forests, hills, and ravines. The park surrounds the Cuyahoga River.

Central Plains

Western Ohio has rich, fertile soil. Many farms are located in this region, and they grow corn, soybeans, and other crops.

Climate

Ohio has cold winters and hot, humid summers. There is a large amount of snow in the winter. For many years, Ohio has struggled with spring flooding. Since the early 1900s, Ohioans have widened riverbanks and constructed dams and reservoirs to help manage spring floods.

Average winter temperatures in Ohio range from lows of 16° Fahrenheit to highs of 37°F. The coldest recorded temperature in Ohio was −39°F on February 10, 1899, in the town of Milligan. The warmest recorded temperature was 113°F on July 21, 1934, near Gallipolis. In general, northern Ohio has a mild autumn.

Average Annual Precipitation Across Ohio

The average annual precipitation varies for different areas across Ohio. What problems might people have if their area receives too much rain, and what could they do to solve these problems?

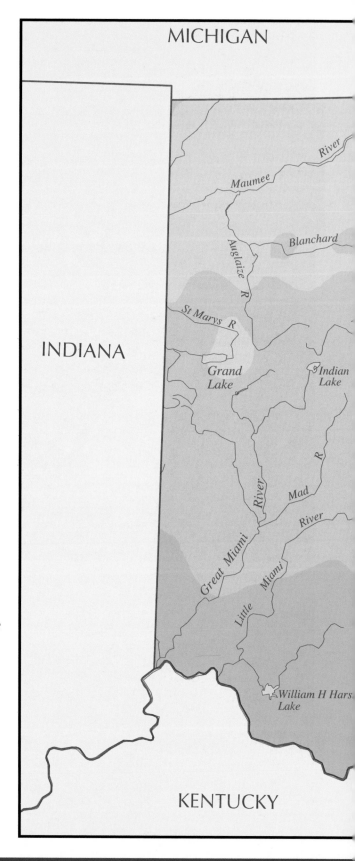

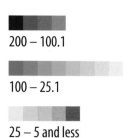

LEGEND
Average Annual
Precipitation
(in inches)
1961–1990

200 – 100.1

100 – 25.1

25 – 5 and less

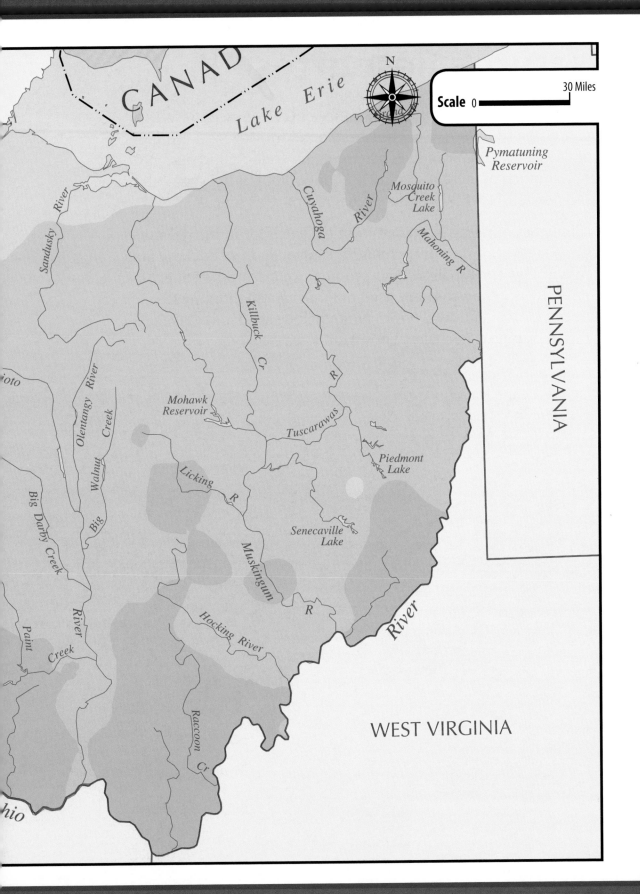

CANADA

Lake Erie

N

Scale 0 ▬▬▬▬▬ 30 Miles

Pymatuning
Reservoir

Sandusky River

Cuyahoga River

Mosquito
Creek
Lake

Mahoning R

PENNSYLVANIA

Killbuck Cr

Olentangy River

Walnut Creek

Mohawk
Reservoir

Scioto

Tuscarawas

R

Piedmont
Lake

Licking R

Big Darby Creek

Big

Senecaville
Lake

River

Muskingum

R

River

Paint Creek

River

Hocking River

WEST VIRGINIA

Raccoon Cr

Ohio

Nature's Resources

Ohioans recognized the importance of their mineral resources during the 1800s. Coal was first found in 1808, and mining soon became a major industry in the state. Today, Ohio does not have as much of these resources as it once did, but the state still has an estimated 11.5 billion tons of coal reserves, as well as oil and gas.

Many other minerals are taken from the earth for industrial use. Ohio's most important mineral is limestone, and the Buckeye State ranks among the top limestone-producing states in the nation. Some types of limestone are used in flooring and monuments. Other industrial minerals from Ohio include sand and gravel, salt, sandstone, clay, shale, gypsum, and peat.

The Ohio River is a major commercial route for distributing goods. The river is an access point for six states.

The state's long Lake Erie shoreline contains some of the area's largest cities and heaviest industry. For many years, the water quality in the lake suffered because of industrial pollution. Fish and bird populations had been steadily declining in these waters until efforts were made to clean the lake. By the early 1990s, recreational fishing had resumed along Ohio's shoreline.

The Cardinal Plant is a coal-fueled power plant. It is located near Brilliant, Ohio.

Most of the limestone that is mined in Ohio today is found in the western region of the state.

Vegetation

From dense forests to open prairies, Ohio's natural vegetation provides habitats for many different types of animal life. Forests in Ohio are mainly found in the state's southern and eastern areas. In most of the state, farmland has replaced the original forests.

Hardwood trees common to the state include oak, ash, maple, hickory, walnut, and basswood. Virginia pine, white pine, and eastern hemlock are some of the **conifers** that grow in the area. The Ohio buckeye tree is found mostly near rivers and in moist areas. It can grow as tall as 80 feet, and it bears yellow flowers in the spring.

Springtime brings a variety of forest wildflowers to Ohio. It is not unusual to spot violets, mayapples, hepaticas, and bloodroot in the spring. In the fall, many wildflowers, such as black-eyed Susans and goldenrods, grow in open spaces.

Butterfly Weed

The butterfly weed, a common wildflower in Ohio, is also called the orange milkweed. It attracts the caterpillars of monarch butterflies, which feed on the leaves.

Northern Blazing Star

The northern blazing star grows best in dry, sunny places. This wildflower is not bothered by heat and drought.

Ohio Buckeye Tree

The Ohio buckeye is Ohio's state tree. Its leaves, stems, and flowers can have an unpleasant odor when crushed.

Red Maple Tree

Red maple trees are found throughout Ohio, in moist areas of open woodlands and along creeks. The tree can grow up to 70 feet tall and 40 feet wide.

Wildlife

Ohio was once home to large mammals such as elk, cougars, black bears, timber wolves, and bison, or buffalo. Today, the white-tailed deer is the only native large mammal that is still plentiful in the state. White-tailed deer were once hunted nearly to extinction, but by the late twentieth century, they were found in every Ohio county. Common small animals in the state include cottontail rabbits, beavers, muskrats, raccoons, moles, and opossums.

Ohio lies along an important bird migration route. As many as many as 400 different kinds of birds spend parts of the year in the state. About 180 bird **species** are native to Ohio, including wild turkeys, quail, and pheasants. There are also many kinds of fish in the state's lakes and rivers. They include bass, northern pike, walleye, and muskellunge. In the north, Lake Erie is home to walleye, steelhead trout, and yellow perch.

White-tailed Deer

The official state animal, the white-tailed deer eats a variety of fruits, nuts, grasses, and leaves. The fur of young deer is covered with white spots, which disappear over time.

Walleye

The walleye, which eats insects and other fish, is a popular game fish in Ohio. The largest one ever caught in Ohio weighed more than 16 pounds and was 33 inches long.

Cardinal

The state bird of Ohio, the cardinal can be found in all of the state's counties. The male, which is a brilliant red, grows to 8.75 inches long. Cardinals eat insects, seeds, and fruit.

Cottontail Rabbit

The cottontail rabbit is found throughout Ohio. It eats a wide variety of plants, including clover and dandelions, as well as corn and the bark of young trees.

Economy

Pro Football Hall of Fame

Visitors to the Pro Football Hall of Fame, in Canton, can learn about the history of football and the National Football League, as well as some of the greats who have played the game.

Tourism

Ohio is full of fascinating sites for visitors to see. The state has four national historical areas that are within the U.S. National Park system. At Hopewell Culture National Historical Park, visitors can learn about the mound-building Native Americans of the Hopewell culture. The other historic sites are the First Ladies National Historic Site, Perry's Victory and International Peace Memorial, and the Dayton **Aviation** Heritage National Historical Park.

The Pro Football Hall of Fame opened its doors on September 7, 1963, and renovated its exhibit gallery in 2009. Cedar Point, on the shores of Lake Erie in Sandusky, is one of the most popular amusement parks in the world. Cedar Point has a beautiful beach, roller coasters, other thrill rides, and a water park, as well as several onsite hotels.

Hocking Hills State Park

This 2,356-acre state park is popular with both campers and hikers. Its features include deep gorges, waterfalls, rock shelters, and forested areas.

Rock and Roll Hall of Fame and Museum

Located in Cleveland, the Rock and Roll Hall of Fame and Museum has exhibits tracing the history of rock music, memorabilia from many singers and groups, and a gallery dedicated to the artists who have been inducted into the hall.

Hopewell Culture National Historical Park

Huge burial mounds built by the Hopewell people are a striking feature of this park. One mound is 2,000 years old, and some of the mounds are 12 feet high and 1,000 feet wide.

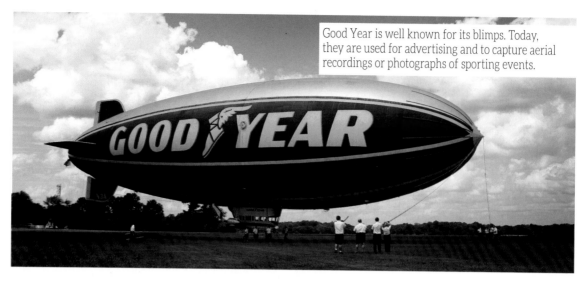

Good Year is well known for its blimps. Today, they are used for advertising and to capture aerial recordings or photographs of sporting events.

Primary Industries

From tires to tractors to automobiles, Ohio's industries keep the nation on the move. Before the onset of **industrialization**, the manufacturing of small-scale farm equipment was one of Ohio's main businesses. Today, Ohio is among the nation's manufacturing leaders. The state is a top producer of primary metals, as well as rubber and plastic products.

Charles Goodyear discovered the process of **vulcanizing** rubber in 1839. The tire and rubber company bearing his name was founded in Akron in 1898, and became one of the state's largest firms. Goodyear, which still has its headquarters in Akron, is the top tire manufacturer in North America and Latin America.

The motor vehicle industry employs many Ohioans. Workers assemble vehicles and shape and stamp metal for automobile parts. Metalworkers also manufacture sheet metal, machinery, and tools. In recent years, more Ohioans have been engaged in the aerospace, aviation, and defense industries. **Biotechnology** is also a growing field.

In 1852, Ohio was the first state to issue laws that protect **working women**.

Ohio's **aerospace industry** earns more than **$8 billion** annually and employs **more than 130,000** workers in Ohio.

Value of Goods and Services (in Millions of Dollars)

Manufacturing makes up a significant part of Ohio's economy. What factors would lead manufacturing to be so important to the state? What types of resources would have to be available in the state for this to occur?

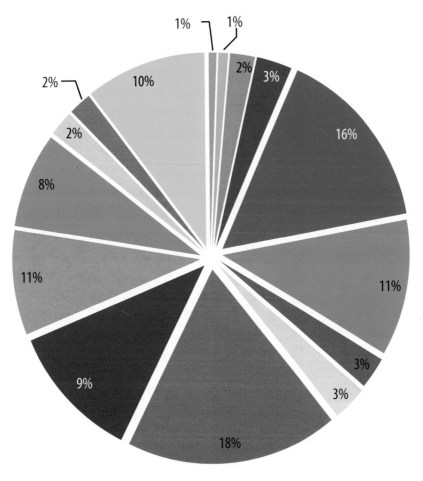

● Agriculture, Forestry, and Fishing $4,262		● Finance, Insurance, and Real Estate $115,251	
● Mining...$5,171		● Professional and Technical Services $72,027	
● Utilities...$13,436		● Education $55,215	
● Construction...$19,007		● Health Care..$50,239	
● Manufacturing $98,693		● Hotels and Restaurants...............................$13,373	
● Wholesale and Retail Trade $71,792		● Other Services $12,327	
● Transportation..$16,943		● Government $65,706	
● Media and Entertainment $18,813			

Goods and Services

Ohio's **civilian** workforce numbers approximately 6 million people. Manufacturing employs about 10 percent of Ohio's workforce. Farming now provides jobs for only a small percentage of Ohio's workers. This was a large shift from the state's early days, when farming was the population's main occupation. The largest segment of the workforce is employed in the service sector, including nurses, schoolteachers, and bankers.

Transportation and shipping are also important in Ohio's economy. Columbus, Cleveland, and Cincinnati are the major trade and transport centers, handling such exports as machinery, transportation equipment, fabricated metals, and rubber products.

Many big name car companies have assembly plants in Ohio. Ford, Chrysler, and Honda are some of the big names found in the state.

Corn and soybeans are Ohio's major crops. Other crops include wheat, hay, tomatoes, apples, grapes, and mushrooms. Ohio is also a major producer of greenhouse and nursery products. Many farms in the state are devoted to floriculture, which is the study of flowers or flowering plants. These farms provide plant bedding, potted flowering plants, and cut flowers.

The Robert Rothschild Farm, known for producing award-winning food products, is located in Urbana, Ohio.

Ohioans have access to a variety of communication services, including many television and radio stations, as well as newspapers. The Cox and Scripps newspaper chains both began in Ohio in the late nineteenth century. The state has also been home to some highly acclaimed editors and journalists.

In 2014, 245 million bushels of soybeans were produced in Ohio.

Hiawatha, a Native American leader, co-founded the Iroquois Confederacy, or the Five Nations.

Native Americans

Among the early Native Americans to settle in the region were those of the Adena culture, which lasted from about 500 BC to 100 AD. The Adena were Ohio's first farmers, and they left behind evidence of agricultural settlements, as well as pottery and large ceremonial mounds that can still be seen today. The Hopewell people, like the Adena, were mound builders who created massive structures for worship and social gatherings.

The Hopewell made ornaments from flint, mica, copper, shells, and animal teeth and claws. They lived in the area from about 200 BC to 500 AD. Another group, the Mississippians, lived in the region until about the 1700s.

The Mingo, related to the Iroquois, lived in the upper Ohio River Valley. The Shawnee entered from the south, and the Miami from the west. The Ottawa and the Wyandot, also called the Huron, came from the north.

Before long, these groups were uprooted and overpowered by the peoples of the well-organized Iroquois **Confederacy**. The confederacy had the first democracy in North America. In the years that followed, the Native Americans experienced conflicts with European explorers and settlers who arrived from the eastern and southern United States.

The Ohio River, as it is today, was an important transport route for Native Americans in the Ohio River Valley.

Exploring the Land

The first European known to have arrived in the Ohio River Valley was the French explorer René-Robert Cavelier, sieur de La Salle. He arrived around 1669 and claimed the entire area for France. The French established fur trading with the Native Americans. Other fur traders, many of them British, began to enter the region in 1685. Missionaries began coming to Ohio in the late 1700s from Germany.

Timeline of Settlement

Early Conflicts

1750 The Ohio Company hires Christopher Gist to survey the land around the Ohio River. Gist provides a detailed description of what is now southern Ohio.

1749 Jean-Baptiste Le Moyne, sieur de Bienville, places a series of lead plates along the banks of the Ohio River to show French ownership of the land.

1754 The French and Indian War begins. The British, helped by some Indian groups, fight against the French and their Native American allies. An important issue is which nation would control the Ohio Country.

1669 René-Robert Cavelier, sieur de La Salle, explores the Ohio River Valley and claims the area for France.

1763 The British win the French and Indian War. They gain control of the Ohio Country.

1763 The British defeat a rebellion led by Ottawa chief Pontiac.

Early Exploration

Conflict over control of the fur trade in the area known as the Ohio Country was one of the causes of the French and Indian War. Great Britain won this war, between France and Britain, in 1763. During the American Revolution, battles were fought in the Ohio area. After the Revolution, the territory became a part of the United States.

1790–1794 Settlers and Indians engage in a series of battles, ending with the signing of the Treaty of Greenville in 1795.

Territory and Statehood

1788 Members of the Ohio Company of Associates found Marietta, the first permanent settlement in the region established by people of European descent.

1802 President Thomas Jefferson signs the Enabling Act, calling for the admission of Ohio as a state as soon as possible.

1803 Ohio becomes a state.

1787 The U.S. Congress passes the Northwest Ordinance, establishing the Northwest Territory, which includes Ohio.

1770 Missionaries arrive from Germany and establish several missions in what is now Ohio.

Missions and Early Settlements

1812–1813 Ohio is the site of important battles during the War of 1812, including the Battle of Lake Erie.

Migrants from New York, the New England area, and Pennsylvania were the first to settle in Ohio.

The First Settlers

Americans from the eastern United States began settling the Ohio area soon after the American Revolution. One of the first acts of the new U.S. government was the Northwest Ordinance. The law opened the area north and west of the Ohio River to orderly settlement.

In the early 1800s, settlers came from Germany, Ireland, France, Scotland, Wales, Great Britain, and Sweden. Many Amish and Mennonite settlers came from Switzerland. Ohio's fertile farmlands also began to attract people from other parts of the United States. While New Englanders settled in southeast Ohio, eastern Ohio attracted Quakers from the South and Mid-Atlantic regions. Other people living in the South, including many African Americans, settled in central Ohio. Today, there remains a strong southern influence in parts of Ohio.

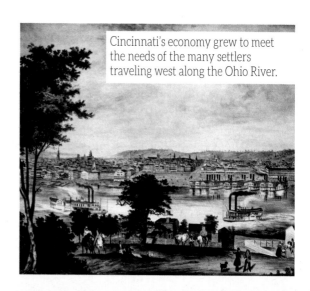

Cincinnati's economy grew to meet the needs of the many settlers traveling west along the Ohio River.

Several **utopian** groups established small, tightly knit communities in Ohio in the early 1800s. One well-known group was the Shakers, a Christian **sect** that attracted followers in the United States in the late 1700s. The Shakers believed in living together without showiness in small farming communities. Another utopian community was that of the Zoarites, a German group that believed in sharing property and responsibility equally among all the members of a community. Their Ohio village, Zoar, lasted from 1817 until 1898.

Ohio has the largest Amish community of any state in the U.S., with more than 69,000 Amish residents.

Today, visitors can experience the preserved town of Zoar. Tours and demonstrations are available to guests.

History Makers

Many notable Ohioans contributed to the development of their state and country. Seven U.S. presidents were born in Ohio, more than any other state except Virginia. Prominent Ohioans also include other political leaders and activists for equal rights, some of the nation's leading inventors, and more than 20 U.S. astronauts.

Thomas Edison (1847–1931)

Thomas Edison was born in Milan. He was extremely curious as a child and invented his first device, to transmit telegraph signals, when he was 16. When he was 21, he set up a research laboratory in New Jersey, where he and his employees developed many inventions. These include the incandescent electric light bulb, the phonograph, the carbon microphone, and the kinetoscope, which is a type of motion-picture projector. By the time he died, Edison held the **patents** on 1,093 devices.

William Howard Taft (1857–1930)

William Howard Taft was born in Cincinnati. After graduating from Yale University and Cincinnati Law School, Taft served as a prosecutor and judge. He became Secretary of War in 1904. A Republican, Taft was elected president in 1908. As president, he took steps to limit the power of big business. Taft ran for reelection in 1912 but lost. In 1921, he became chief justice of the U.S. Supreme Court. He is the only person in U.S. history to have served as both president and chief justice.

John Glenn (1921–)

John Glenn was born in Cambridge. In 1959, he was chosen by NASA, the National Aeronautics and Space Administration, as one of the first seven U.S. astronauts. On February 20, 1962, he became the first American to orbit Earth. Glenn represented Ohio in the U.S. Senate from 1975 to 1999.

Carl Stokes (1927–1966)

Carl Stokes was born in Cleveland. He was elected to Ohio's House of Representatives in 1962. Five years later, he was elected mayor of Cleveland, becoming the first African American mayor of a major U.S. city. He was elected to a second term. After leaving office, he served as a television newscaster, a judge, and a U.S. ambassador.

Neil Armstrong (1930–2012)

Neil Armstrong was born in Wapakoneta. He studied to become a fighter pilot and a test pilot. He became a NASA astronaut in 1962 and flew his first mission four years later. In 1969, Armstrong commanded the Apollo 11 moon landing mission. During the mission, on July 20, he became the first person to set foot on the Moon.

Culture

Ohio residents can enjoy many music festivals throughout the year, including the Jazz Picnic in the Courtyard at the Cincinnati Art Museum.

More than 916,000 visitors went to the Ohio State Fair in 2014, a new state fair record.

The People Today

More than 11.5 million people call Ohio home. About 85 percent of the population is of European heritage. African Americans make up about 12 percent of the population, and small numbers of Asian Americans and Native Americans also live in the state. Some of Ohio's African Americans are the descendants of escaped slaves who made it safely out of the South before the Civil War via the **Underground Railroad**.

Hispanic Americans, who may be of any race, make up about 3 percent of the population. Many early **immigrants** arrived in the northeast region from Russia, Eastern Europe, and Italy. Many of these immigrants came to Ohio to work as laborers, often draining swamps and building canals.

The University System of Ohio includes 13 four-year universities and 23 two-year community and technical colleges. One of the main schools in the system is Ohio State University in Columbus, which was founded in 1870. Other state schools are Miami University, Kent State University, and Bowling Green State University. Private schools of higher education include Oberlin College, Antioch College, and Case Western Reserve University.

Ohio's population **increased** by more than **18,000** people from 2000 to 2010.

Q What are some of the reasons many people from other states and countries are choosing to move to Ohio?

State Government

Ohio's government, like the federal government of the United States, is divided into the executive, the legislative, and the judicial branches. The executive branch, led by the governor, is responsible for making sure the laws are carried out. The governor and lieutenant governor serve four-year terms.

The House of Representatives has 99 members who are elected to two-year terms. The Senate has 33 members who are elected to four-year terms. Together, they form the General Assembly of the Legislative Branch, which creates Ohio's laws. The judicial branch interprets laws and governs the court system. Seven judges rule on cases in the state's Supreme Court, which is the highest court in the state.

William McKinley, the 25th president of the United States, who was born in Niles, was one of Ohio's most famous political figures. Elected in 1896 and again in 1900, McKinley expanded U.S. territory overseas during the Spanish-American War. Another notable political figure in Ohio politics was John Mercer Langston, who is believed to be the first African American elected to public office in the United States. In 1855, he was elected town clerk of Brownhelm. He later served in the U.S. House of Representatives.

The Ohio Statehouse was completed in 1861, after 38 years of construction delays.

Ohio governor John Kasich was elected governor in 2010 and reelected in 2014.

John Mercer Langston began his political career in Ohio in 1855. He was one of the first African Americans elected to public office in the U.S.

Ohio's state song is called **"Beautiful Ohio."**

Beautiful Ohio I sailed away;

Wandered afar;
Crossed the mighty restless sea;

Looked for where I ought to be.

Cities so grand, mountains above,
Led to this land I love.

Beautiful Ohio, where the golden grain

Dwarf the lovely flowers in the summer rain.

Cities rising high, silhouette the sky.

Freedom is supreme in this majestic land;

Mighty factories seem to hum

in tune, so grand. Beautiful Ohio, thy wonders are in view,

Land where my dreams all come true!

* excerpted

The Cleveland World Festival celebrates the city's diversity. It highlights more than 120 different ethnic groups.

Celebrating Culture

Ohio played an important role in the Underground Railroad and the **abolitionist** movement. Anti-slavery feelings in Ohio during the early 1800s helped ignite the Civil War, resulting in the end of slavery. John Rankin, a Presbyterian minister in Ripley, believed deeply in abolition and helped many slaves escape. He formed the Ohio Anti-Slavery Society in 1835, and with his family and neighbors, he helped as many as 2,000 people escape bondage.

At Cleveland's African American Museum and at festivals throughout the state, African Americans celebrate their culture. Ohio State University hosts a large African American heritage festival every spring. This festival is a week-long celebration that features African and Caribbean food, music, and poetry.

The John Rankin house was one of the best documented and most used Underground Railroad stops.

The first Mennonite and Amish settlers arrived in the early 1800s. More Mennonites and Amish followed, often transplanting existing communities from Pennsylvania. Many others immigrated directly from Switzerland or elsewhere in Europe. Today, Mennonite groups live in communities across the state, and about one-fourth of all Amish people in the United States live in Ohio. The Amish believe in distancing themselves from the outside world. Members are not allowed to participate in wars or hold public office. They follow a simple, farm-based lifestyle and avoid technology such as electricity, telephones, or automobiles. The followers of the Mennonite faith, on the other hand, tend to be less strict about the use of technology.

Mennonite and Amish communities are mostly centered in the rural areas of the state.

The Amish community in Ohio is mostly centered in Holmes county. Visitors to the area can view the Amish lifestyle and purchase quality Amish goods.

The Cleveland Orchestra is nearly 100 years old. It performs in Cleveland, Florida, and Vienna.

Arts and Entertainment

Many acclaimed writers have hailed from Ohio. One noted writer who lived in Cincinnati in the 1800s was Harriet Beecher Stowe. She was the author of the novel *Uncle Tom's Cabin*, which raised awareness of the evils of slavery. President Abraham Lincoln is said to have called her "the little woman who started the big war." Other famous Ohio writers include Pulitzer Prize and Nobel Prize winner Toni Morrison, humorist James Thurber, novelist Sherwood Anderson, poet Rita Dove, and children's authors R. L. Stine and Dav Pilkey. Author Zane Grey is best known for his novels and stories set in the Old West.

Long before becoming the *iconic frontman* of the rock and roll band **The Foo Fighters**, and drumming for **Nirvana**, **Dave Grohl** was born in Warren, Ohio in 1969.

The **Grammy award**-winning hip-hop group **Bone Thugs-n-Harmony** is from Cleveland, Ohio.

Film director Steven Spielberg was born in Cincinnati. He has directed some of the most successful films in history, including *Jaws*, *E.T.*, and *Jurassic Park*. Many actors and actresses hail from Ohio, including television stars Ed O'Neill, Sarah Jessica Parker, and Drew Carey, as well as Oscar winners Halle Berry and Paul Newman. Musicians with Ohio roots include the rap singer John Legend and the singers Bow Wow, Tracy Chapman, and Macy Gray.

E.T. made almost $800 million worldwide.

Three-time Grammy Award winner John Legend was born in Springfield, Ohio, in 1978.

Nearly 15,000 people attend the Midwest Outdoor Experience in Dayton, Ohio, each year.

Sports and Recreation

Ohioans, as well as visitors to the state, have a variety of outdoor activities from which to choose. With the state's wealth of natural areas and state parks, many people enjoy camping, fishing, canoeing, and hiking. A popular destination for outdoor enthusiasts is Wayne National Forest, which covers three separate stretches in the hills of southeastern Ohio. The area sits in the rugged foothills of the Appalachian Mountains and has many lakes, rivers, and streams. Adventurers will likely spot wildlife, including deer, wild turkeys, and a variety of songbirds, in the region. The sport of spelunking, also called caving, can be done in a number of Ohio's caverns. Spelunkers, equipped with flashlights, descend into caves on ropes or on their hands and knees to explore the caves.

LeBron James began his career with the Cleveland Cavaliers, receiving the **2004 NBA Rookie of the Year**. He was born and grew up in Akron, Ohio.

Russell Wilson, quarterback for the Seattle Seahawks and **Super Bowl XLVIII champion,** was born in Cincinnati, Ohio. He was the *first* freshman quarterback to have the honor of being named the Atlantic Coast Conference's (ACC) first-team All-ACC quarterback.

Ohio boasts a number of professional sports teams. The state has two teams in the National Football League, the Cincinnati Bengals and the Cleveland Browns. Ohio's professional baseball teams are the Cincinnati Reds and the Cleveland Indians. The Reds have won the World Series five times, in 1919, 1940, 1975, 1976, and 1990. The Indians have been Cleveland's team since 1915. They have won two World Series championships, in 1920 and in 1948.

The Cleveland Cavaliers have been Ohio's National Basketball Association team since 1970, while the Columbus Blue Jackets have been the state's National Hockey League team since 2000. Ohio fans also cheer on the state's college teams. The Ohio State Buckeyes have been especially successful in football and men's basketball.

The Cincinnati Bengals have played in the Super Bowl twice in the team's history. Their first appearance was in 1981.

Ohio's NHL team, the Columbus Blue Jackets, play at the Nationwide Arena. Their uniforms were inspired by Ohio's Civil War history fighting for the North.

Get To Know
OHIO

The city of **TWINSBURG** hosts the annual **TWINS DAY FESTIVAL** every spring, inviting twins to take part in a parade and other events.

OHIO'S STATE INSECT is the **ladybug.**

Harry M. Stevens created the FIRST HOT DOG in Ohio in 1900.

The state beverage is **tomato juice** because Ohio once produced more tomato juice than any other state in the country.

Akron, Ohion, was the first city to use police cars, in 1899.

EACH YEAR, 1.1 MILLION OHIO SPORT FISHERS SPEND AN ESTIMATED **$1.1 BILLION** ON **FISHING.**

The Cincinnati Reds were the first professional baseball team in the United States.

Brain Teasers

What have you learned about Ohio after reading this book? Test your knowledge by answering these questions. All of the information can be found in the text you just read. The answers are provided below for easy reference.

1 What is the capital of Ohio?

2 Which large body of water borders Ohio to the north?

3 Who was the first European to travel through the Ohio River Valley?

4 Who were Ohio's first farmers?

5 What year did Ohio become a state?

6 Which common Ohio wildflower attracts the caterpillars of Monarch butterflies?

7 Which Ohioan wrote Uncle Tom's Cabin?

8 What is Ohio's nickname?

ANSWER KEY
1. Columbus 2. Lake Erie 3. French explorer René-Robert Cavelier, sieur de La Salle 4. The Adena 5. 1803 6. Butterfly weed 7. Harriet Beecher Stowe 8. The Buckeye State

Key Words

abolitionist: a person who worked to end slavery in the United States

aviation: the design, development, production, and operation of aircraft

biotechnology: the use of microorganisms or biological substances to perform industrial or manufacturing processes

civilian: not military

confederacy: an alliance between groups for mutual assistance and protection

conifers: trees, such as evergreens and shrubs, that bear their seeds and pollen on separate, cone-shaped structures

game: wild animals hunted for food or sport

glaciers: large masses of slow-moving ice

immigrants: people who move to a new country

industrialization: the process of switching from an agricultural way of life to mechanized industry

patents: legal documents giving the person who invented something the sole right to make or sell it

reservoirs: lakes, often artificial, for collecting water

sect: a group of people with the same beliefs who follow the same leader

species: a group of animals or plants that share the same characteristics and can mate

Underground Railroad: a secret network in the United States in the 19th century that helped slaves escape to freedom

utopian: believing in the possibility of building an ideal place with a perfect social system

vulcanizing: making rubber hard and durable enough to use for vehicle tires

Index

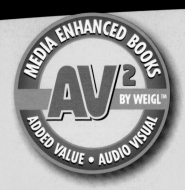

Log on to www.av2books.com

AV[2] by Weigl brings you media enhanced books that support active learning. Go to www.av2books.com, and enter the special code found on page 2 of this book. You will gain access to enriched and enhanced content that supplements and complements this book. Content includes video, audio, weblinks, quizzes, a slide show, and activities.

AV[2] Online Navigation

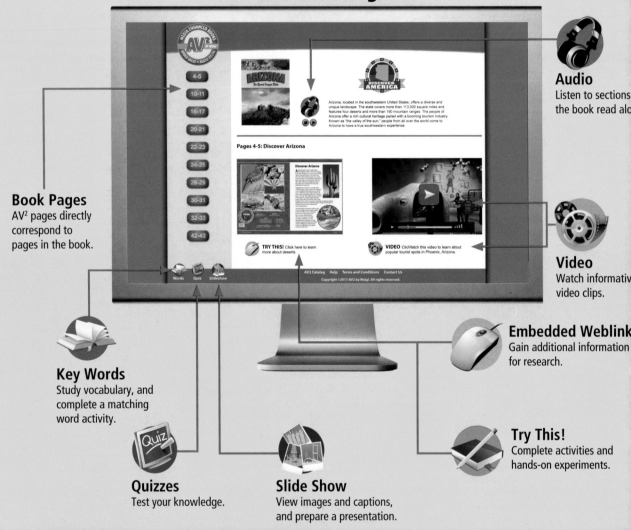

Audio
Listen to sections
the book read alo

Book Pages
AV[2] pages directly
correspond to
pages in the book.

Video
Watch informativ
video clips.

Key Words
Study vocabulary, and
complete a matching
word activity.

Embedded Weblink
Gain additional information
for research.

Try This!
Complete activities and
hands-on experiments.

Quizzes
Test your knowledge.

Slide Show
View images and captions,
and prepare a presentation.

AV[2] was built to bridge the gap between print and digital. We encourage you to tell us what you like and what you want to see in the future.

Sign up to be an AV[2] Ambassador at www.av2books.com/ambassador.

Due to the dynamic nature of the Internet, some of the URLs and activities provided as part of AV[2] by Weigl may have changed or ceased to exist. AV[2] by Weigl accepts no responsibility for any such changes. All media enhanced books are regularly monitored to update addresses and sites in a timely manner. Contact AV[2] by Weigl at 1-866-649-3445 or av2books@weigl.com with any questions, comments, or feedback.